T-MAX
Excited to Teach You
CREOLE

Jinia Nelzi

NEWMAN SPRINGS PUBLISHING
320 Broad Street
Red Bank, NJ 07701

First originally published by Newman Springs Publishing 2021

ISBN 978-1-64531-129-4 (Paperback)
ISBN 978-1-64531-130-0 (Digital)

Printed in the United States of America

To Rose Marie and Jean Simon Nelzi

My mom is from Haiti which is an island in the Caribbean. They speak French and Creole. Creole is the mother language which means the first language which you speak at home. French is the studied language which you learn in school. I only know Creole because that's what Mom teaches me. My dad is American. He was born and raised in America in the state of Florida just like me. He only speaks English, though. I like speaking two languages because I can say things two different ways.

If I want to ask your name I would say:

What is your name?
And in Creole I would ask
Ki jan ou rele.

My name is T-max
Non mwen se T-max
It's really Maxime like my father's, but everyone calls me T-Max, which means Little Max.

Would you like to learn some Creole?
I can teach you to speak some Creole.

Repeat after me.
I have two eyes.
Mwen gen de je.

I see with my *je* my mom is making cookies.

I have two ears.

Mwen gen de zorey.

I can hear with my *zorey* my mom whisking away the dough to make some cookies.

I have only one mouth.
Mwen gen yon sel bouche.
I can't wait to taste with my *bouche* the yummy
cookies my mommy is about to bake.

I have only one nose.

Mwen gen yon sel nen.

I can smell with my *nen* the cookies are
baking, and they smell really, really good.

I have two hands.

Mwen gen de men.

I can't wait to hold soft cookies in my *men*.

I have two feet.

Mwen gen de pye.

I use my *pye* to run to my mom when she says the cookies are ready.

I love cookies a lot.
Mwen renmen bon bon anpil!

I got to go the cookies are ready!
Mwen gen poum ale, bonbon an pare

Bye
M'ale

Sounds in Creole

A sounds like a short *O*
Like the *O* in *O*ctober

E like short *A*
Like the A in *A*pple

I sounds like a long *E*
Like the E in *E*asy

O sounds like long *O*
Like the O in *O*boe

U sounds short *I*
Like the *I* in *I*t

About the Author

Jinia Nelzi was born and raised in United States to Haitian parents Jean Simon and Rosemarie Nelzi. Jinia grew up in a household where speaking Creole was a must. Jinia attributed learning to speak, read, and write the language to church, trips to Haiti and working at her mom's shop where she had to translate the prices her mom said to their English customers. With nieces and nephew growing up in the United States to English-speaking parents, she sees it's harder for them to be interested in learning Creole. Jinia is hoping that the stories on T-Max will encourage other children whose parents just don't only speak Creole or know someone who does to spark the interest to learn the language.